The Spelling Bee and Me

A Real-Life Adventure in Learning

Gail Small
Kendra Yoshinaga

Illustrated by David Endelman

Rowman & Littlefield Education
Lanham, Maryland • Toronto • Oxford
2005

Published in the United States of America
by Rowman & Littlefield Education
A Division of Rowman & Littlefield Publishers, Inc.
A wholly owned subsidiary of The Rowman & Littlefield Publishing Group, Inc.
4501 Forbes Boulevard, Suite 200, Lanham, Maryland 20706
www.rowmaneducation.com

PO Box 317
Oxford
OX2 9RU, UK

Copyright © 2005 by Gail Small and Kendra Yoshinaga

All rights reserved. No part of this publication may be reproduced,
stored in a retrieval system, or transmitted in any form or by any
means, electronic, mechanical, photocopying, recording, or otherwise,
without the prior permission of the publisher.

Small, Gail, 1947–.
    The spelling bee and me : a real-life adventure in learning / Gail Small, Kendra Yoshinaga ;
    illustrated by David Endelman.
        p. cm.
        ISBN: 978-1-57886-257-3
    1. Spelling ability—Testing. 2. Spelling bees—United States. 3. Yoshinaga, Kendra.
    4. National Spelling Bee (2004) I. Title.

LB1574.S58 2005
372.62'2—dc22

                                                                    2005042901

⊖™The paper used in this publication meets the minimum requirements of
American National Standard for Information Sciences—Permanence of
Paper for Printed Library Materials, ANSI/NISO Z39.48-1992.
Manufactured in the United States of America.

Authors' Dedication

We dedicate this book to every child who has bravely attempted to spell words known and unknown. You are all champions~just for trying!

Illustrator's Dedication

Dedicated to those who enjoy the play of words.

I like exploring in my yard,
watching the bees gathering nectar, working so hard.
My dog chases bunnies, birds, and squirrels.
My brother and I swordfight and whirl.

Wherever I go, I leave a trail of socks and toys.
My sister's different~books are her joys!
She devours them all, like a vacuum I think.
She whizzes through them and gives me a wink.

We all learn in our own special ways.
Reading's how she learns spelling, every day.
She reads here and there, on the floor, in a chair,
in the bed, in the car, in the bathtub, anywhere!

She reads everything, she never stops,
For her it's great fun~reading is tops!
She always aces her spelling tests.
She craves more words than all the rest.

Before each holiday, her class holds a bee,
so each student can learn to perform worry-free.
I thought there'd be bees buzzing around,
but the ring of a bell was the scariest sound.

A bee is a gathering of minds joined as one,
a community sharing learning and fun.
The spellers have books with colors so bright,
some study all day and into the night.

Sis said, "Spelling's great, so where is the bee?"
Competition one was at the library.
Each contestant was a VIP,
who tried their best, it was plain to see.

The kids were all friendly, and wished each other luck.
The bee words were spoken, and then some got stuck.
The spellers were smart, and tried to think quick,
but she won the bee, with the word "caustic."

School winners tried hard at the Area Bee,
where each was a champ, we all could agree.
My sister was granted a very fine wish,
and won this bee with the word, "knish."

Spellers came from all around,
to the County Bee, with words profound.
It took three hours, then with grace and finesse,
she won this bee with the word, "manes."

Being up on the stage is like being up at bat.
Bases loaded, two outs, ball three and that's that.
You hit a home run if you spell the word right,
you've scored in the game~you're in the spotlight!

It took her three bees to get to D.C.
She worked really hard, and studied with glee.
She quizzed her daddy and bounced on the bed,
while visions of spelling words danced in her head.

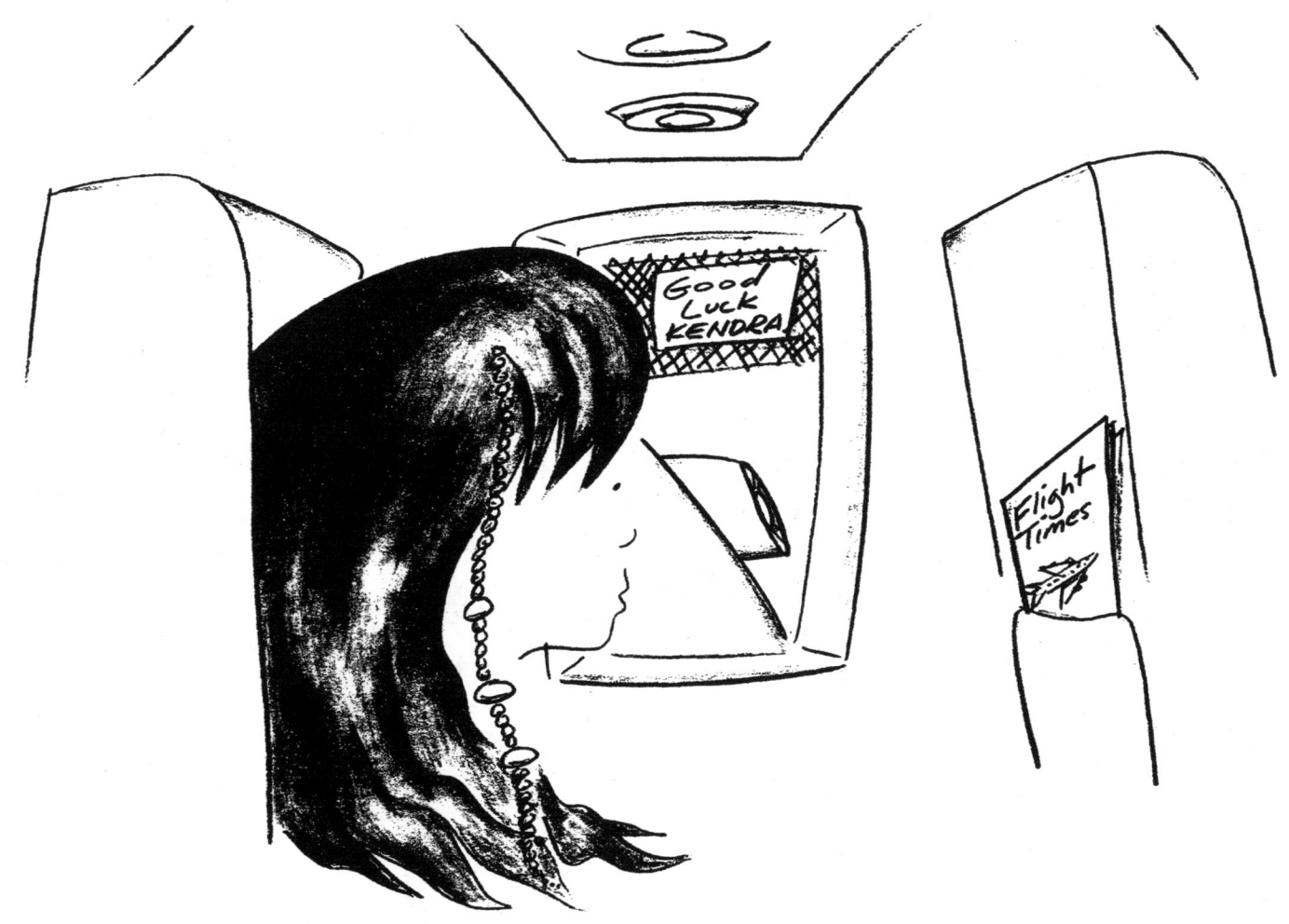

We flew to D.C. and landed at night.
The sparkling monuments were lit up so bright.
It was more than spelling~new sights to see,
friends to make, places to be.

In a big hotel it all took place.
Spellers from everywhere came for the race.
With different backgrounds, accents, and colors of eyes,
contestants came in every size.

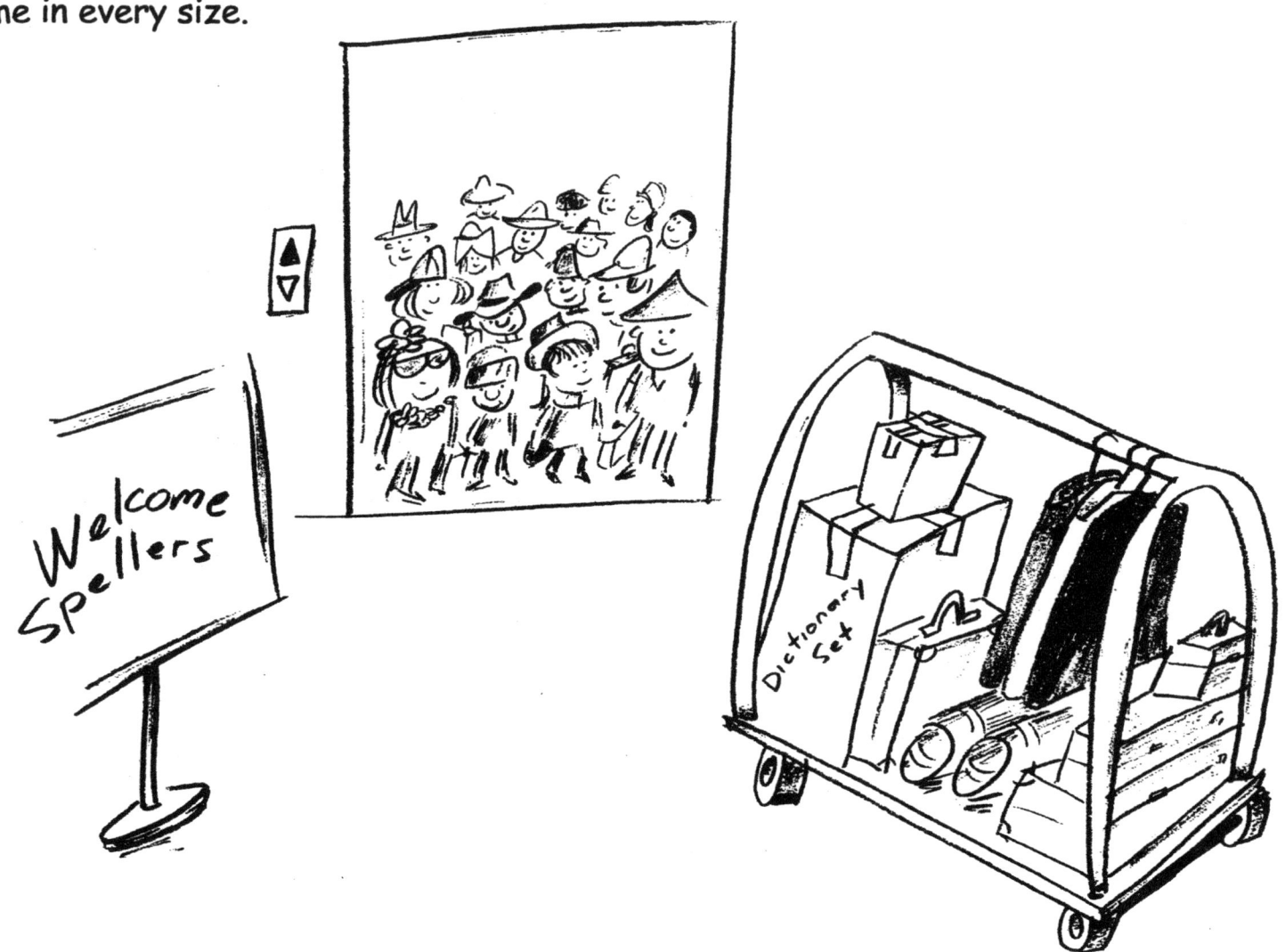

And so did the spelling words~long and short,
from modern and ancient tongues and tort.
French, German, Latin, Greek, Portuguese,
Persian, Hebrew, Latin, Japanese.

Families came along~like me and you,
brothers, sisters, grandparents, too.
When sis was on stage I couldn't make a sound,
until she spelled and finished her round.

Then everyone clapped and I did too.
We applauded everyone and never said boo.
I watched and listened and wiggled my feet.
A national spelling bee is really neat.

Even for siblings just like me,
who try to remember i before e,
except after c~some words disagree,
like ancient, you see.

The spellers asked questions to gain hopeful clues,
like origin, definition, and how is it used?
Everyone tried and a few of them cried.
I'll bet their brains got really fried.

The announcer declared when the word had a homonym,
a sound-alike word that's not a synonym.
What part of speech the speller could ask,
noun, verb, or adjective to help with the task.

Multiple pronunciations and definitions help too.
The word in a sentence brings it clearly in view.
The speller may pause and write in the air,
in hopes that the word would magically appear.

*L*isten...

*T*hink!

Follow Every *C*lue

More than spelling is what you do~
listen, think, follow every clue.
Think hard, think fast, keep your head clear.
Focus on the word, the answer is near.

The clock ticks down~so the speller begins.
There's loud applause~as each one wins.
We all hold our breath~"Repeat the word please."
Some spell them wrong and others with ease.

They walk up to the microphone, adjust it to size,
all of them hopeful, their eyes on the prize.
A bee is like a roller coaster ride,
bumpy and twisting, the audience on your side.

Wondering, waiting, and sounds fill the air.
Silence, clicking of cameras, bright lights everywhere.
Step by step and one word at a time.
Spell it right, to the next level you climb.

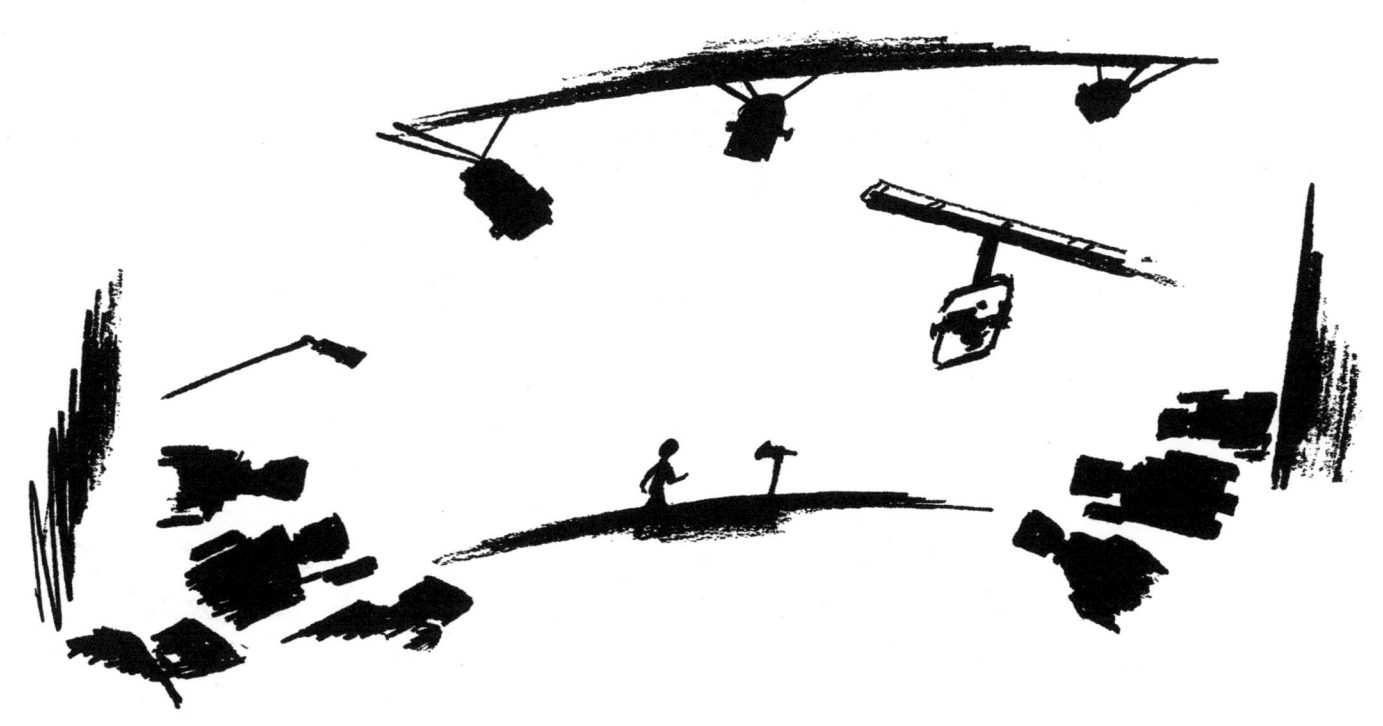

Musical chairs is a game I love to play.
In the bee they get to play it every day.
Every time I looked they took another chair
~a bell would ring and they wouldn't be there.

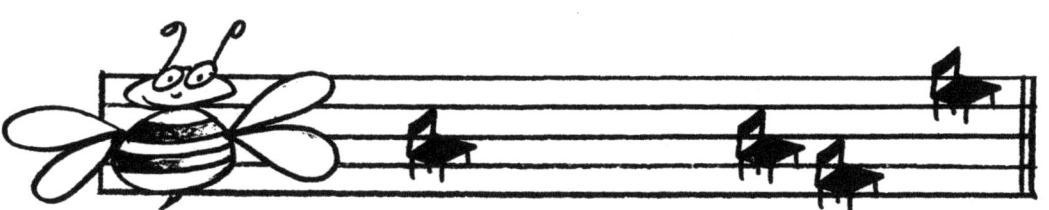

The room was capacity~someone in every seat,
waiting to witness the final feat.
In the very last round there stood only one,
who had to spell twice to prove they had won.

The room was so quiet, I could hear my heart beat.
The crowd jumped up and I climbed on my seat.
There was loud applause and a big grin on all.
The winner's trophy was shiny~and very tall.

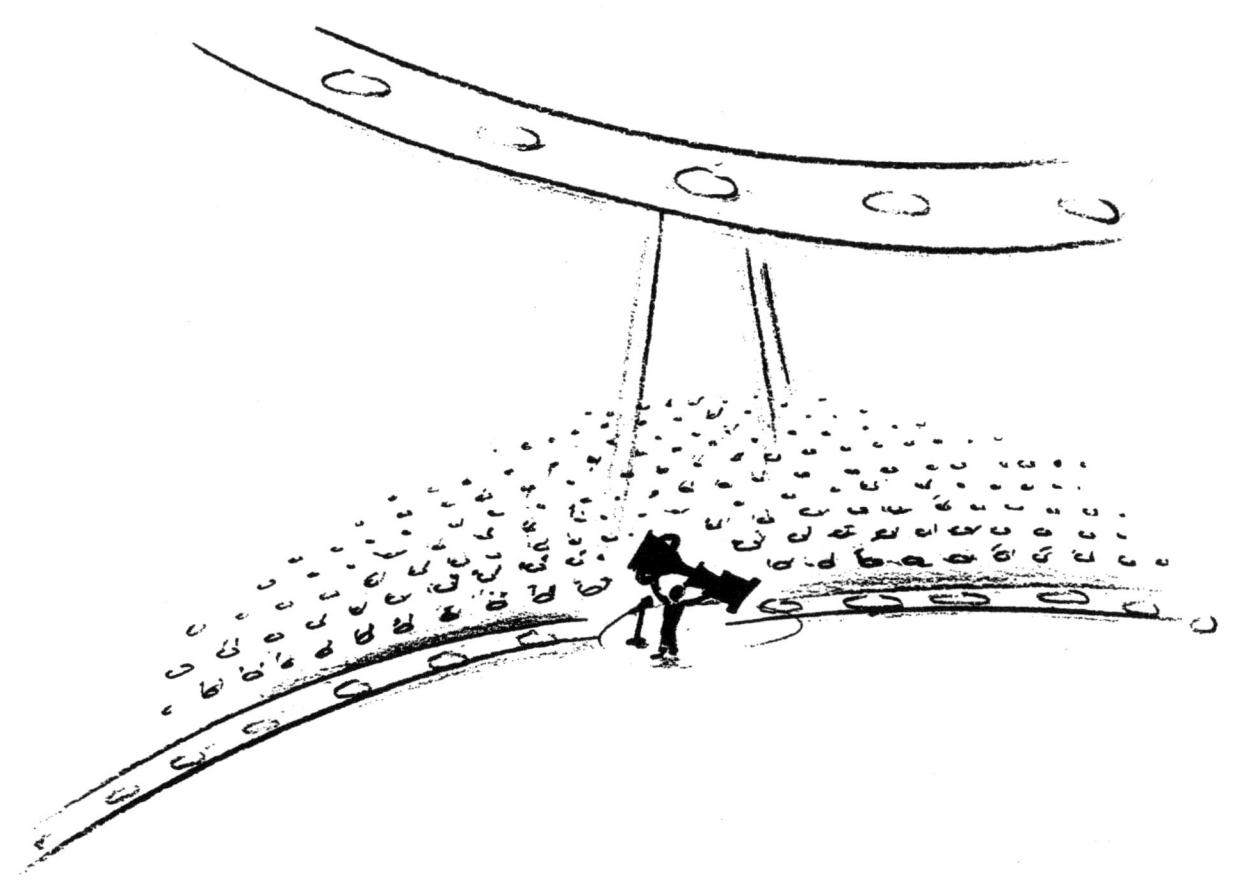

The last night was a party to celebrate and smile.
New friendships and memories were shared for awhile.
Spellers talked of "hope to see you next year,"
as they returned to home states~there was many a cheer.

With high hopes and goals the spellers compete,
not knowing which words they will meet.
Each felt great about doing their best.
They achieved and accomplished, which was the real test.

Words, meanings, and definitions blend together as one.
Putting together these pieces is the point of the fun.
Spelling's like an ice cream sundae crowned with a cherry,
with tasty treats, like fudge and strawberry.

And who wouldn't dream to return?
To go to a national spelling bee~is a lot to earn.
Perhaps someday the contestant I'll be,
with my dictionary in hand, on the way to the bee.

Don't Worry, Bee Happy

Special Spelling Tips Section

Thoughts from Dad

Dr. Steve Yoshinaga, Kendra's Coach

Kendra had been anxiously anticipating her first official spelling bee season for some time. Since her teacher, Ms. Gail, conducted spelling bees monthly and on holidays, she was in almost 25 class bees during first, second, and third grade, and she won them all. Being in a mixed grade classroom, she had outlasted older children who, in some instances, later won the school spelling bee in the years before Kendra was eligible to participate. Even as a third grader, Kendra was one of the best spellers in school, but she was always too young to participate and unable to show it.

I was a complete spelling bee novice, as I had never witnessed Ms. Gail's class spelling bees, let alone the media coverage of the National Spelling Bee. When Kendra began winning Scripps Spelling Bees, we were stunned, as we didn't have expectations of her winning anything in this first official year. Maybe that was why it was such a magical spelling bee season. Kendra achieved so much without any expectations.

Kendra is a prolific reader, and her wonderful memory allowed her to remember many of the words she had read. She knew almost all of the beginning Paideia words without having to study them. In addition, Kendra is extremely poised onstage~a valuable attribute in the spelling bee world. Every speller struggles to keep their composure, but Kendra's concentration helped her focus. Furthermore, Kendra's early successes in Ms. Gail's spelling bees inspired her to work hard to achieve at this higher level. It was Kendra's resolve, not her parents', that drove her to accomplish what she did this year. Although young, she has many characteristics that help her succeed in spelling bees. Yes, my job as coach was easy with this talented young girl. Even so, only others who have prepared diligently for a spelling bee can appreciate what a spelling competition entails. All of the painstaking preparation and natural talent are at the mercy of a careless mistake or the chance of the draw. No matter what happened with Kendra, she was a winner to me. She learned how to pace her studying and achieve very lofty goals.

A spelling bee is not just about spelling words. It's about thinking on your feet while in front of many people. It's about figuring out how to spell words from what you know, remembering things in the past. It's about listening to what the pronouncer says, and not hearing what you want to hear. It's about figuring out what the pronouncer wants to say, even though he or she may be pronouncing it wrong. It's about knowing the difference. It's about all of these things at the same time. I can only imagine that being able to figure out a word you have never heard of, while in front of live television, and a crowd of hundreds, is an amazing feeling.

By the time Kendra went to the County Spelling Bee, she had learned all of the Paideia words. Barring a careless mistake, she was prepared to go all the way through the Paideia. If they did leave the Paideia, and she missed an off-list word, she could still hold her head up high, as mastering the Paideia's 3,700 word list was quite an accomplishment.

Throughout the County Spelling Bee I tried to remain calm, but it was hard. During one intense moment, I chanced to look over to my left and a fellow dad (who I didn't know) caught my attention and clutched at his heart. He seemed to know what I was feeling. When Kendra sealed her win with her final word, she made a little hop to the side, clinched her fists, and burst into a huge smile. The room launched into a standing ovation. She had survived a 3-hour, 44-round marathon of a spelling bee, the longest in county history, and she won after just turning 10 years old! I was beyond thrilled. I was cathartic. At round 35, I lost control of sequential thinking.

Kendra became an instant local celebrity. Her photo was on the front page of several local newspapers. Many groups and politicians acknowledged her accomplishments and love of reading and spelling. Kendra was walking on a cloud. All of her hard work and ubiquitous reading were paying off.

The National Spelling Bee brought more pride. Kendra had studied hard for this competition, but exhaustive study for this top level of spelling competition is almost impossible. In her first year of competition, we knew she couldn't do all the studying it takes to win a National Spelling Bee. However, she wanted to give it her best shot, so we had an aggressive study plan that she completed with days to spare. She made me proud just in the way she prepared for this open-ended competition. Her training, coupled with her excellent memory and composure, helped her tie for 27th at the 2004 National Spelling Bee. This is 27th out of around 10 million kids who started the year hoping to win their school spelling bees! The high placing, beyond my expectations, helped me to realize that she is competitive at the national level in spelling. And she is so young!

Surpassing Expectations

Kendra far exceeded our expectations at many levels. In each spelling bee she was one of the youngest spellers, and with returning spelling bee champions present, it was hard to have high expectations. We hope she did her best and enjoyed herself. We set aggressive study goals appropriate for each spelling bee level and she exceeded those goals. I remember that both times she achieved her study goals a couple of days before each competition. There was something reassuring about knowing she prepared as well as she could for each level. It was calming for both Kendra and her parents and coaches.

Unforgettable Memories

I had many precious moments and feelings this year. Feeling the good-natured competition at all levels of spelling bees was a great pleasure. Everyone appeared to be on a common mission to defeat the dictionary, not each other. The friendly sportsmanship demonstrated by the County Spelling Bee runner-up stands out among a number of outstanding displays of sportsmanship. Knowing Kendra prepared well for the bees lessened the stress for us and gave me a strange calming feeling. I vividly remember my disbelief when Kendra won the County Spelling Bee after hours on a spelling rollercoaster. I also relished that many family, friends, and complete strangers were cheering for our 10 year-old. Most importantly, I felt happiest that one little girl discovered her gift and a way to share it with the world.

Preparing for the Spelling Bee Season

If you have a young child that wishes to prepare for the local spelling bee, here are some suggestions that may help him or her.

Getting Started Early with the Official Spelling Word List, the Paideia

Find a previous year's official spelling list, or Paideia (pronounced pie-day-ah), by contacting your local sponsoring newspaper. Your spelling bee coordinator, or a competitor from last year, may have an extra copy. The Paideia has approximately 3,700 words, arranged in subject categories, and within the particular category, by degree of difficulty. Historically, only 10 to 20% of the Paideia is changed from year to year. Find the sections newly introduced in the last two years and use the beginning and intermediate words as a guide for vocabulary building during the summer and fall. This will help in your preparation for digesting the new Paideia words.

When the new Paideia words come out, start by memorizing the beginning words in all the categories. The final goal is to know all the words in the Paideia. However, one should start with all the beginning words, then once mastered, move to the intermediate and advanced words. Although there are a wide variety of spelling bee formats at the school or local level, the best formats use the Official Pronouncer's Guide to help direct them to a given set of words. It is the job and responsibility of the local spelling bee coordinator and the spelling bee sponsor for that area or region to determine the spelling bee format. The Official Pronouncer's Guide includes a recommended subset of words from the Paideia in order from least difficult to most difficult words. WARNING~the Official Pronouncer's Guide is only available to pronouncers and spelling bee officials, and a speller will be disqualified if it is determined that they have obtained or seen this guide.

The methods for learning the Paideia words differ with each individual. Drilling and typing and/or writing the words are major aspects of Kendra's study methods; however, learning the correct pronunciation and definition should occur as soon as possible. The Paideia words, with their correct pronunciations and definitions, are available online. Listening to the correct pronunciation is good practice for spelling bees. In local spelling bees, one has to be careful of alternate pronunciations. It is important to learn the definition of the word, usually the main definition used in Webster's 3rd New International Dictionary. It does not happen often, but if a word sounds unfamiliar, knowing the definition may help in spelling it.

Drilling Tips

Beginning Words

While drilling, the coach should have access to a good dictionary and the Paideia. Most of the beginning words are familiar; therefore, pronunciation of the words should not be difficult. However, if an unfamiliar word appears, then the dictionary should be able to help the coach with the pronunciation. Be sure to know the correct pronunciation of each word. If you are unsure of a pronunciation, find it in the Audio Paideia and attempt to learn its definition. If you, or your coach, have a hard time with the pronunciation, it is possible that the spelling bee pronouncer may also struggle with the pronunciation. Knowing the definitions of these hard to pronounce words may help in identifying a mispronounced word in a spelling bee.

Intermediate Words

The best resources to have available are the Paideia Dictionary, Webster's 3rd New International Dictionary, and the Audio Paideia. Another excellent resource is the online version of Webster's Collegiate Dictionary and the electronic version of Webster's 3rd. The online Collegiate Dictionary has access to oral pronunciations and sometimes includes both primary and alternate pronunciations.

Advanced Words

The pronunciations of many of the advanced words are indeed challenging for the typical person, so do not fret if you are stumbling through them. Difficult words can be identified during the drilling and lists made of them for specific drilling sessions. In addition, difficult words can be studied in word searches, crossword puzzles, or handwriting practice. There are convenient websites that allow one to make word searches, etc., with specific lists of words. Exposure to difficult words in any manner is beneficial.

Work on beginning words first, intermediate next, and then advanced words. Some sections within the Paideia are not categorized as such, but instead have intermixed 1, 2, and 3 designations. Learn these in ascending order, essentially treating "1" as beginning, "2" as intermediate, and "3" as advanced words. Local spelling bees can be very different, but generally the words are asked in increasing levels of difficulty. Some local spelling bees don't get past the beginning words, while others are quite advanced. Know the precedents of your most recent local spelling bee by asking lots of questions, especially of your local spelling bee coordinator, and set your study goals appropriately.

For advanced spellers whose aspirations are to compete nationally, mastery of the Paideia words is imperative. Once this is accomplished, the student has to study for "off list" words. The only limitation of "off list" words is that the word has to be in Webster's 3rd New International Dictionary (and the addendum too!). Therefore, study beyond the Paideia is open-ended, unless one can master all the words in Webster's 3rd, that is, over 500,000 words! However, there are hopeful strategies. Further study might include reading the National Spelling Consolidated Word Lists that are available online. These are extensive lists of frequently, moderately, and infrequently used words in spelling bees. We also had fun finding short lists of specific types of words, for example, types of phobias, double letter containing, or Yiddish words. Many advanced spellers also spend time learning about prefixes, suffixes, and roots of words. Understanding the parts of words, and how they are put together, may help in deciphering unfamiliar words in a spelling bee.

Our local spelling bee coordinator was a fountain of spelling bee knowledge. She helped me form realistic goals for each spelling bee, but always warned me that, in spite of great preparation and intentions, "Anything can happen!" We found that to be very true this year. One slip of the tongue, one frozen moment, or one unfamiliar word, can take anyone out of a bee. It is tremendous stress that is unforgiving of a mistake. These and many other warnings made me wary of this spelling bee world, but it was Kendra's interest that drove our interest, not her parents' desire for her to excel in that arena. It is important that the speller understands and accepts what is involved at each level of study and preparation. The speller is the driver and the coach sets the course.

Exercises

- Listen to the Audio Paideia
- Drill with Audio Paideia

- Drill with coach

- Read the words out loud

- Write or type Paideia words

Exercise

Listen and Type or Write the Words

Have the computer on the Real Audio Player window with the appropriate Audio Paideia category queued. Have the Paideia words available but partially covered with a card. Type or write the words along with their pronunciations and definitions. Check your spelling, then correct if necessary. Start and stop playing the Audio Paideia, depending on whether you can keep up with the typing or writing, then correcting, of the words.

Strategies

- Break up work into sections

- Work on beginning, then intermediate, then advanced words

- Pace yourself

- Start ASAP

Be Best Prepared to Approach Goals

1. Take baby steps, but take lots of them.

    a. Make schedules that break up large goals into small chunks.

    b. Don't procrastinate; there are lots of words in the Paideia!

2. Prepare early for spelling bee season.

    a. Work on returning Paideia sections in the summer.

    b. Get ahead in non-bee subjects during non-bee season.

3. Integrate the subjects~overlap non-bee subjects and activities.

    a. e.g., A Language Arts project on a particularly interesting Paideia category.

    b. e.g., or handwriting practice with difficult Paideia words.

4. Have fun!

Realistic Goals

Set reasonable goals, no one needs to know all of the Paideia words immediately!

Examples of Realistic Goals

1. Listen to 7 of 28 beginning sections of the Audio Paideia by the end of the week.

2. Finish drilling once through the entire Paideia beginning words by the end of the month.

3. Learn all of the beginning words and half of the intermediate words by the first spelling bee.

4. Learn all of the intermediate words by the second spelling bee.

Thoughts from Mom: The Emotions of a Spelling Bee

Dr. Brenda Yoshinaga

Can you imagine your child in the National Spelling Bee? It was an exhilarating experience for our whole family! The nervousness, the highs, and the almost inevitable "DING" of the bell~all combine to whip up emotions into a frenzy. No wonder it is essential to keep your perspective and those of your speller in mind. Of course, getting to the national level means winning smaller, local spelling bees. If you cannot locate a local spelling bee for your speller, call the education departments of your local newspapers to find out whether they sponsor a spelling bee. Your local school districts may also hold spelling bees.

When you begin to read and hear about the national contestants, it appears that every speller at the National Spelling Bee is an incredibly talented academic achiever! This is true~every one of the spellers is a winner! Your speller is now among a rarefied group. Just making it to this level defines your child as a winner~no matter whether the bell dings sooner or later~or maybe never, for the champion. It is important to reassure your speller that they are already a winner, and this is the icing on their cake of success.

Of course, you should try to help your speller prepare for the competition, so they feel ready for the event. Aside from studying the entire Webster's 3rd New International Dictionary, a Herculean task, you can make sure that your speller has the Paideia and extra word lists well under control.

Before you arrive in Washington, D.C., it is important to consider the needs of your child. Adequate sleep is imperative. If you will be crossing a number of time zones, you may want to acclimate your child to the new time zone in the week or so before the spelling bee. Jealously guard your speller's rest~if others are sharing your room, just say, "lights must be out by 10."

On the days of competition, avoid the hustle and bustle of the breakfast crowd, and instead pick up something to go or order room service. Let your speller choose where to go for lunch and/or dinner. Don't make them study all the time~let them relax, too! Due to nerves, you may wind up ordering food, watching your speller pick at it listlessly, and then throwing it out. Just be sure that your speller has eaten something~complex carbohydrates (a bagel) and some protein (milk) will help.

Decompressing is an important part of the day. My daughter liked to jump on the bed while she spelled words. During the competition, I saw some kids discreetly playing with silly putty, as a vent for nervous energy. In the second round, the speller sitting next to my daughter had a tiny rubber pig. My daughter looked over in curiosity, and the girl placed the pig on the tip of her finger and said, "Oink, oink!" They both quietly giggled, enjoying the release of tension. However, the vast majority of the spellers have exquisite composure, and at most, you may see some fiddling with their placards.

Many spellers have a "lucky" talisman, such as a sweater, a piece of jewelry, or other such item. Perhaps they were wearing it when they won their local spelling bees. However, if your speller starts to get overly focused on their "lucky" item, remind them that it was their hard work that got them this far~nothing else (besides your support, that is!).

If and when your speller gets "the bell," be there for them. Let them talk. Reassuring words and hugs will help. When my daughter got dinged in the fifth round, she didn't shed a tear. She had surpassed her expectations and knew she had done her best. After a cookie and a soda, she had regrouped and realized that the pressure was off. Now we had to go back to the ballroom to see how our new friends were doing!

How do you raise a child to withstand the academic and psychological pressure of a spelling bee? Preparation is key, but there's more to it than the Paideia. Every child is different, but here's how we've tried to encourage our kids. We hardly ever watch T.V. We occasionally enjoy shows about nature and history. But I generally regard T.V. like a sugary treat, and rarely indulge. I don't think the popular cultural icons are healthy role models, especially for girls, who may view the rail-thin, made-up divas as ideals to mimic, leading to low self-esteem and even eating disorders. We visit our local library almost every week, and return with great treasures! My daughter also participates in a book club, where the girls meet once each month with a library volunteer who guides the discussion. Games also help children develop the skills they need to appropriately react when they lose~and when they win. This is part of developing compassion and recognizing the needs of others. Consider volunteering with your child in a situation where they can help others who are less fortunate.

I think many small successes build up inside children to help them face bigger challenges with grace and composure. These "small successes" could be gained through music recitals, sports events (games, karate tests, etc.), or even by reading a passage at your church or temple. Practice generates confidence, which can be carried on to the next challenge. I also believe we need to set strong examples for our kids to follow. Watching mom or dad prepare to face their challenges appropriately will teach your child how to face their own challenges.

Creative Ideas For Teaching Spelling: Spelling Can Be Fun!

Ms. Gail Small, Kendra's First, Second, and Third Grade Teacher

To me, spelling is more than a piece of paper, a pencil and a list of words to study. When I was in school I did my homework, got an "A" on each spelling test, and truthfully, forgot the words the very next day. When education becomes interesting and fun, the curiosity and challenge stimulate the learner to explore and take extra steps forward. Included below are tips and tricks that I have used with my students and the school spelling bee champions to make spelling become a part of a child's everyday world.

Spelling Bees

Besides incorporating a multitude of varied activities to stimulate student interest and retention in spelling, having frequent bees is a novelty that grasps students' focus and fosters retention. Students line up for fun and to see if they can still spell their most recently studied "words." When performed on a regular basis, without any real "winner," students share the task of asking each other for the words that are to be spelled. Spelling can be mastered merely by hearing peers spell words with varied levels and meanings. A comfort level develops without a fear of defeat. Cheers are given in support of correctly spelled words, as well as effort. Word recognition and vocabulary accumulate with time. Children begin not only to seek more difficult words in their spelling, but also to discover their definitions, pronunciations, rules, and origins.

Look Up and Learn

Over the years some visitors in my classroom curiously inquired, "why are they looking on the ceiling?" Just as others also asked, "why do you have so many school spelling bee winners?" All of these creative ideas for teaching spelling lay the foundation for developing a confident speller. Ask children to help you write words on colorful poster paper and place the posters high on the ceiling. The practice of writing words is valuable. You might want to color code the words so they are significant (such as study level or component/multi-syllable/foreign origin). I always make lists of the "most misspelled words." Children who often say, "I'm done with my work~now what do I do?" have time to relax and learn. My students sat comfortably on beanbag chairs or even lounged on the floor and focused on the ceiling. This is such a nonacademic method that works. When students see the words, they are processing them. When they repeat the process over and over, they own the words. Using multiple creative methods, rather than just a paper and pencil, develops the speller in all of us.

My most vivid recollection of Kendra, at the young age of 6, was when she would look up to the ceiling, scrunch her nose and with a knowing smile master the spelling of new words. You could almost see the wheels turning and the inspiration in place as she would independently walk across the classroom. She would stand on her tiptoes to reach for a pile of dictionaries so she could search for new word meanings that further built her vocabulary.

Word Find

Write vocabulary words or "spelling" words neatly on a piece of paper (wall, chart, or poster board). After the words are written and spelled correctly, camouflage the words by placing random letters to blend in all around them. Writing the words in itself is a study technique. Identifying words is fun and increases recognition, retention, and mastery.

Dkfhtoeowpdlg**spelling**gndkgghdokeidspp

Example: defdkfhtls**is**jhdkejthekslekee

Keid**a**dhfklethdldl**good**lllfh**thing**llpl

Spello?

Write words on a blank grid. Each participant writes the words in any square of their choice. The leader of this game then calls out the words. Players cover each word with a marker. Bingo rules are flexible. The real winner is every participant, because they have not only written the words themselves, but actually heard the words and looked to locate them on the game grid.

Card Game

Write words on index cards or cardstock. Make four of each word to create a set of four matching word cards. Create rules for a "fish" type game. Players are writing, seeing, and saying the words repeatedly throughout the game.

Game Board

Draw a colorful game board with blank spaces on a path. Use an original pattern or one that is similar to a favorite game. On each space, write words that are being studied. Include difficult words that will be mastered through playing games. Include words by category, alphabetically, level of difficulty, or randomly to seek mastery.

Dictionary Race

Separate the children into groups. Give each group words at their level of challenge and ask them to find the words in the dictionary. It becomes a "contest." Not for the win, but the fun of finding words. The skills of using guidewords and alphabetizing become strengthened as children race to find the words.

Silly Story

Children can write a story using given words. Make it a silly story. Laughter is healthy and spelling is too.

Musical Story

Play fun music with a peppy melody. Place a piece of paper on each desk. Have children write a word or brief sentence and when the music stops, everyone changes seats! As they sit down at a new seat it is then their assignment to expand the sentence or story. Continue this activity to make learning come alive as children change seats while playing this game. There is no "win" or "lose" in this learning game. It is action while listening, absorbing, increasing vocabulary, learning editing skills, and having fun. Help them correct any spelling errors, not for a "grade" but for recognition of accurate spelling. For a fun review, print out the final collaborative stories for all to enjoy.

Find Words

Ask individual students or groups to find a new word for every letter of the alphabet. Make it "an alphabet book" and include words of increasing difficulty as you play this regularly. Together, students can read or trade wordlists and help each other to increase their vocabulary.

Write It All Wrong!

This one is the most difficult for me. It is not easy to write every word wrong. The children love it! They have to find your "mistakes." Scramble the letters in words and encourage students to find each word and then write it correctly.

The Printed Word

Class newspaper? School newspaper? Individual stories or books in the works? These exercises will help students expand their vocabulary and acquire the editing process. The edited, final copy reflects the pride of a finished product, is well worth reading, and will be cherished as a keepsake. Students have come back as adults to say this taught them the most.

Build a Ladder

Make a list of words on a ladder-type drawing. Begin with words with the fewest letters and increase the list to words with a multitude of letters. This is a visual experience to see many words of different lengths.

Create a City

It is easy to collect and clean empty milk cartons, containers, and empty boxes. Students can write words on them. Create a village or city with words. The various boxes can be covered and decorated artistically, as the written words on each become known and owned. We once changed a city monthly. Each month it had a new name, theme, and location. Where in the world were we, anyway? Also each month the level of difficulty increased in terms of the words spelled and the vocabulary used in the unique display.

Music Anyone?

Ask children to write words in poetry or in a song. Some of the most difficult spelling words become fun through sounds and repetition. Those words will remain in their brains forever! Students have returned years later recalling,

"Do you remember?" and sing me some crazy original song with a knowing smile. Several have shared that the words have appeared on a college entrance test, and under the pressure of sitting in a test, they could barely contain their laughter. This can also be applied with nonsense songs about syllables and parts of speech. As in "I~~ am a Verb." The movement is always fun, although it can't be used, I'm sure, in any college entrance process!

Sandbox

Writing words while pulling fingers through the sand, seeing them, saying them, feeling them is a playful beginning and introduction to words.

Glitter

Discover new words by writing in glue. Pour on the glitter and enjoy spelling and reading words with some extra pizzazz. Kendra even brought pixie dust to the spelling bee and sprinkled it all over us!

Chalk/Water Play

Have your speller write words in chalk or paint them with water on a sidewalk or driveway. This is a beneficial visual method that's messy and fun!

Toothpicks/Popsicle Sticks/Straws

Arrange sticks to make letters and words. Later you can glue them on paper to save and see newly created words.

Dice

Throw dice, and whatever number comes up, spell a word with that many letters, sounds, or syllables. Get or make several blank dice or cubes. Write alphabet letters on each side. Throw the dice and spell or create new words. Find them in a story or dictionary.

Crossword Puzzle

Make a grid with squares. Include spaces to fill with words that read up and down as well as across. Write definitions on a separate page and fill in the spaces. Use challenge words with unusual spellings and new definitions to increase spelling and vocabulary levels.

Artful Spellers

Look at a word and cover it with your hand or a fun, colored marker. Uncover parts of each word as you say and spell them. Say the word aloud and spell it so it is heard. Write the word with yarn, glue, or something that fingers can touch and feel. Look at the word and say it. Use the words for decorations to see and review.

Teach young spellers the vowels, consonants, and rules. As their skill levels increase, be sure to include nouns, blends, plurals, suffixes, silent sounds, syllables, and homophones.

ABCs

Alphabet cereal, cookies, or soup noodles are a fun way to identify letters and words. Freshly washed hands can create edible words (or for a longer-lasting lesson, you can glue them). I have also made bread, cookie, and pretzel dough that roll out nicely into words. The smell of something freshly baked is divine, and, the longer the words, the more to eat! If you're not into food, make the nonedible "bread dough" ornaments. Write meaningful words or new words to make ornaments for display or to give as gifts. And, you never know, one of those "words" could even be the winning spelling bee word!

In the same way, have children cut out letters or small words from colorful magazines and used greeting cards. Teach the children to arrange them together to make a collage of both familiar and new words. Help them to understand that making mistakes is a discovery method to create new words. As fingers arrange and rearrange letters, a nearby dictionary is a valuable tool to master unknown words as well as to seek out meanings to increase vocabulary.

Make Lists

Children making lists is a part of the learning process. Whether it is a list of words to incorporate later into a poem or story, or a list of what I want for breakfast or snack, the lists will be read and reread. How about a list of make-believe wishes? Cities I have heard of? States? Places? Jobs people can do? Favorite colors? Things I want in a catalog? Movies I want to see? Costume choices for Halloween? Food for a special holiday or outing? Making the list is not as important as reading words, strengthening vocabulary and incorporating writing, word recognition, and spelling into daily activities.

I Love the Thesaurus

Do any of the above with a thesaurus! Ask students to find alternate words for those selected in any activity. A thesaurus strengthens and expands a student's mastery of the English language. Multiple meanings become part of children's daily language and conversation.

A Letter to Kendra

Dear Kendra,

To see you standing up on the stage amidst judges, bright lights, cameras, and a full audience was awe-inspiring even to me, who knows you so well. Your composure, confidence, smile and the twinkle in your eyes caught the hearts of many.

To be able to spell a word by simply knowing the language of origin and a brief definition of the word, is indeed an art. It is not just your mastery of vocabulary and the English language. It is your attitude and the ability to soar in all avenues of academia.

While spelling is the subject of the spelling bee, the interactions between contestants are a lesson as well. Each of you demonstrated immeasurable skills: those of compassion, understanding, and empathy for your fellow contestants from all walks of life and locations.

Congratulations!

Ms. Gail ;-)

A Message From Kendra

Kendra Yoshinaga, 10-Year-Old National Spelling Bee Contestant, 2004

You see, where I live they wouldn't allow me to participate in an official school spelling bee in third grade, since the minimum grade was fourth. You've got to be kidding me! I always believed that it didn't matter what you looked like, or how young or old you are, you can do anything if you put your mind to it. Unfortunately, some people didn't agree. So, I decided to make lists on my own out of the Paideia. The time came when I walked into a library, where my first "official" spelling bee was held, as "the new girl," and walked out as "the girl who won the spelling bee." "Caustic" was my winning word, and I walked out on clouds.

Then I started studying for the next "official" spelling bee level. When the day came, I felt comfortable yet nervous sitting in a chair on the stage of a church where it was held. Finally it was my turn. "The word is awmboosh," said the pronouncer. "Awmboosh? WHAT!!!!????!!!!" my mind screamed. But I asked calmly, "May I please have the definition?" The pronouncer said, "awmboosh means to produce in relief usually by stamping on paper or other impressionable surface." I was completely lost here, until I saw, in my mind's eye, the name of a kit my mom gave me for Christmas a few years ago~Fancy Embossment. Slowly, I put two and two together. He means "emboss"! Just then the judges conferred and the pronouncer corrected himself, "It's emboss, I'm sorry."

Now confident, I rattled off the six letters, "E-M-B-O-S-S." "That is correct," said the head judge, and I returned to my seat. Soon, there were no other contestants other than myself and another girl, a lanky seventh grader, who towered above me. We went back and forth for several words and the microphone went up and down. "Palladium," said the pronouncer. "Palladium? Palladium. P-A-L-A-," (I flinched), "D-I-U-M. Palladium." I heard her say. The crowd gasped as the judge shook her head sadly. I walked up to the microphone, adjusted it two or three feet down to my size, and the pronouncer said, "Knish." Knish? Great! I knew that one! "Knish. K-N-I-S-H. Knish." The audience burst into applause, and I was on my way to the County Spelling Bee, but only after my family and I had a little "knish party" with Ms. Gail. We were all delighted and they tasted so yummy. I suppose we had a special reason for them to taste so great!

The County Spelling Bee

Since I did not think I would win the County Spelling Bee, I studied as hard as I could. My dog Yuki was my sweet, faithful study companion. She snoozed and snored next to me while I studied. When the fateful day came, I sat on the twelfth seat of a half-circle of eighteen seats at the City Hall. All of the other contestants seemed to tower over me! "Weapon," said the pronouncer. "Weapon. W-E-A-P-O-N. Weapon." The pronouncer nodded and I quickly sat down, relieved. That was my first word. When it was finally down to the girl from the local Junior High and me, the judge announced that they were going out of the Paideia and into extra words. "Decile. D-E-C-I-L-E. Decile," I said uncertainly. The judge nodded. I sat down happily. She got "apoplexy" right, and I got "cryophilic." "Cryophilic, C-R-I-O-P-H-I-L-I-C. Cryophilic." I heard a ding and sat down disappointed. I heard "pilosity" in some distant corner of my mind. Then I heard what could have been the euphony of my life~I heard the ring of a bell. My opponent missed her word, I was back in. We followed this pattern for the most rounds in history for the County Spelling Bee. Eventually she got "chevesaile." Unfortunately, she spelled it "chevasaile." Ding. "Kathak" said the pronouncer. "Kathak. K-A-T-H-A-K. Kathak." The audience clapped and I remained onstage for what might be the final, winning word. "Manes," the pronouncer said. "Manes?!" Manes is a tough word, but the version I spelled is pronounced "mawn-ez" and means "the spirits of the dead in ancient Roman belief." "M-A-N-E-S. Manes!" So, with those five letters, I was on my way to the national championship in Washington, D.C.~yeah!

The National Spelling Bee

Since I only had two months to study for the National Spelling Bee, I crammed as much as I could. The day finally came. I slept on the plane to Baltimore. Then we caught a taxi to Washington, D.C. My most vivid memory of that trip was when we turned a corner and I saw, brilliantly lit on either side of me, the Capitol and the Washington Monument. We checked into an incredibly huge hotel, and I fell in love at once with the escalators, elevators, and especially the piano in the middle of the pool. Since we had arrived at about 1:00 a.m. eastern time, we checked into a room and fell asleep quickly.

It was a little strange talking to reporters from different newspapers and the radio, because people I didn't know wanted to know all about me. I had just turned 10 years old, and they asked me: "How do you study?" "What do you study?" "How long do you study?" "Do you do anything else but study?" The truth is that I didn't study every minute. I liked exploring new places and that helped me decompress.

Round 1

This day started with a twenty-five-word written test. I sat down at a long table, equipped with a test form, two pens, and a tiny piece of green construction paper and some tape to cover my name. I daydreamed about theme parks and roller coasters. Soon the test started. "Separate," I heard. I quickly wrote it down. "Tofu." The first twelve words were fairly easy, but the thirteenth, "triskaidekaphobia," elicited a collective groan. I knew "triskaidekaphobia," got a lucky guess on "rhinorrhagia" and "Biedermeier," but mangled "rijsttaffel," "chresard," and "boeotian."

Rounds 2 and 3

In round 2, you would receive three points if you spelled your word correctly. I sat on stage waiting for the word, and when my turn finally came, I got "pyrrhotism." I was thrilled and relieved when I got the word pyrrhotism, because I thought of my friend all the way across the country and her bright red hair. "Pyrrhotism! P-Y-R-R-H-O-T-I-S-M." The judge nodded yes and I walked back to my seat.

When round 2 was over, the director announced the names of the spellers advancing to round 3. I sat with my family and Ms. Gail in eager, nervous anticipation. The numbers were announced in random order. It was nerve-wracking! When my number was announced, "21," I felt like I could flip over backwards. I wanted to dance around the room when they said my number~21.

Round 3

When round 3 started, I listened to the words they were giving other spellers, "Telefacsimile? Isochronous? Peritonitis?" They sounded hard. When my turn finally came, though, I got "flibbertigibbet." "Flibbertigibbet? F-L-I-B-B-E-R-T-I-G-I-B-B-E-T. Flibbertigibbet." I sighed in relief and walked back to my seat. As it turned out, a national news program showed a clip of me spelling "flibbertigibbet."

Round 4

In round 4 I was very nervous. I remember telling my mom, "See you backstage," just before heading on stage. When I was on stage I was a bit calmer before hearing the words they were giving out. Strepitous? Panary? Oh, no. I sat waiting for the word that would become either my all-time favorite or least favorite word. I walked tentatively up to the microphone. "Ullaged." I felt a wave of relief. "Ullaged? U-L-L-A-G-E-D. Ullaged." I walked what seemed like an immeasurable distance from the microphone to my chair. Yeah! I had made it to the Championship Rounds!

Championship Rounds

Round 5 started way too quickly~at least for me. All too soon, I was walking up to the microphone, and I heard the pronouncer say, "Nigerois." "May I please have the definition?" I asked. A Nigerois was a person from Niger. "Any . . . alternate definitions?" I heard myself ask. No alternate definitions, I heard. I started spelling. "Nigerois. N-I-G-E-R- . . . O-I-S- . . . E? Nigerois?" The audience sat in silence. There was not a sound in the room, just me and the microphone. Thinking . . . wondering . . . and . . . the dreaded bell rang.

Kendra's Inside Thoughts

I was really excited and a little nervous. When I stand up at a spelling bee I look at a spot on the wall or something interesting so that I am not distracted. At the National Spelling Bee, I focused solely on the pronouncer so I didn't have to see the twenty zillion cameras and all of those people. It always seemed like forever until I got my word, but when I finished spelling my word, time seemed to fly. I said good luck to the spellers around me. We were never against each other~we were allied against . . . the dictionary!

I was 9 at my first official spelling bee. When I first began in the National Spelling Bee, I wore purple, which was the color I wore at all of my previous bees. I brought a little pink bag given to me by my auntie and I carried it everywhere. I do not think anyone could have had more glitter on than I did. I sprinkled pixie dust all over my hair for good luck. Once, I clapped my hands over my brothers, who were patiently sitting in the audience. They didn't know they were glittering until someone asked them, "How much pixie dust did you put on?"

There was something special about meeting other spellers, former champions, and new friends from around the country. We shared camaraderie and supported each other. People I didn't even know wanted me to sign autographs. This was the first time I ever signed autographs. Even when walking in public places, I heard my name, "Kendra." My brain was about to pop. Sometimes there is no more room in my long-term memory. We called home on cell phones and sent e-mails to keep everyone at home up-to-date on the events of the day. I was happy to call home, and I especially missed Yuki. I got to eat lots of good food. The restaurants served chicken nuggets in funny shapes. We had s'mores where you dip cookies and marshmallows into hot melted chocolate. Going out to dinner was part of the spelling bee experience, because I could giggle and have fun. I chilled out because you can't study all of the time!

When I studied using a laptop, I enjoyed changing the font and color as I stared at the words. Ms. Gail was so surprised to see how I practiced, especially when she saw me jumping up and down on my bed as I spelled words out loud. My family was there for me, even my brothers, big and little. They insisted that they hated every minute of the whole experience, yup, but I know differently. I caught them smiling, and waiting, a lot, and watching. I squeezed little Kai and he even let me. He shared my joy by not kicking my shins.

Just so you know~I was number 12 in the spelling bees in California, in the National Spelling Bee I was number 21, and Ms. Gail's favorite number is 3, (1+2, 2+1).

I was amazed when I came home and got so much attention. When my family first drove up to our house there was a huge banner on our front fence, 12 feet long, with signatures, encouraging messages, happy sketches, and other nice stuff from so many people.

Inside Tips

If you learn all of the word roots, then you can form words to insult your brothers and they won't know what you're talking about. I feel superior when I can call my big brother Cory something and he says "huh?" He can't even pronounce it right when he runs to my parents. I can stump mom and dad now and run away in peals of laughter and glee. I am watching for new words all the time. I am reading vocabulary builders and everything in sight. Next time I will study more, but not very differently. Toward going to the spelling bee, I know there was a lot more I could have studied. I've been working a lot harder now, and I hope I'll get a chance to go again. It was a blast!

About the Authors

Gail Small is a Fulbright Memorial Scholar and People to People Ambassador. She has been named to Who's Who In American Colleges and Universities, Who's Who Among American Teachers and is fully certified with The William Glasser Institute. She has been featured at national and international conferences on the subjects of communication, self-esteem, creativity, and gifted and challenged children. As an educator of 35 years, consultant, author, and motivational speaker, Small's goal is to reach children, parents, and teachers throughout the world. She is the author of *Joyful Learning: No One Ever Wants To Go To Recess!* (ScarecrowEducation, 2003), *Joyful Parenting: Before You Blink, They'll Be Grown* (ScarecrowEducation, forthcoming), *The Big Squeal~A Wild, True, and Twisted Tail* (ScarecrowEducation, 2005), and *Cocoon 101* (ScarecrowEducation, forthcoming).

Kendra Yoshinaga is an avid reader who enjoys language arts and is concerned about the environment and world peace. Her hobbies include playing the violin, sewing, bicycling, swimming, writing, drawing, skiing, playing with her pets, and photography. A chipper 10-year-old, Kendra looks forward to competing in future spelling bees.

About the Illustrator

David Endelman's cartoons have appeared in local newspapers as well as national and international publications. His interest in graphics range from cartooning to cartography to computer generated fine art. The art in this book was created with a few pencils and lots of smiles.

www.ingramcontent.com/pod-product-compliance
Ingram Content Group UK Ltd.
Pitfield, Milton Keynes, MK11 3LW, UK
UKHW050008230326
469204UK00014B/348